The American Marten

The American Marten

by **Denise Casey**

Illustrated with color photographs
by **Tim W. Clark and Others**

A Skylight Book

DODD, MEAD & COMPANY
New York

PHOTOGRAPH CREDITS

Thomas M. Campbell, III, pages 14, 30, 59 (top and bottom); Denise Casey, 10, 48; J. Pissot, 50; Roger A. Powell, 18; William J. Zielinski, 28, 33 (top). All other photographs are by Tim W. Clark.

Published by Dodd, Mead & Company, Inc.,
71 Fifth Avenue, New York, N.Y. 10003
Printed in The United States of America by Horowitz/Rae
Designed by Jean Krulis

1 2 3 4 5 6 7 8 9 10

Library of Congress Cataloging-in-Publication Data

Casey, Denise.
    The American marten / Denise Casey ; illustrated by Tim W. Clark and others.
    p.   cm. — (A Skylight book)
    Includes index.
    Summary: Text and photographs examine the elusive American marten, its history, habitats, and behavior.
    ISBN 0-396-09143-1
    1. American marten—Juvenile literature. [1. American marten. 2. Martens.] I. Clark, Tim W., ill. II. Title.
QL737.C25C376   1988
599.74′447—dc19   87-27532
                                                                                  CIP
                                                                                  AC

To my parents

Contents

Introduction

"Why can't you show me a marten? You're studying them."

"Are you kidding? You'll never see one just walking through the woods. I know people who have lived here in the Park for years who have never seen one."

"Show me their habitat and we'll find one."

"This *is* their habitat, from here to the Arctic Circle. But I'm warning you, you'll never see one."

Dr. Tim Clark was showing his friend around Grand Teton National Park in northwestern Wyoming. Having studied American martens for more than four years, he knew better than to expect one of those elusive, weasel-like mammals just to pop out of the treetops and display himself for a visiting scientist.

But not two minutes after they threw off their packs and sat down on a fallen log, a big marten bounded out of the underbrush and right up a dead pine leaning over their heads. Ten feet above them, the marten abruptly stopped, his pointed face staring earnestly down at them. He was the size of a house cat, and his dark amber fur gleamed in the sunlight, set off by a flame-colored "bib" under his chin. His long, furry tail swished. A minute later, he zipped out to the end of the log for a quick look around, then bolted back down and into the brush.

"Thanks, Tim. I knew you could do it."

Dr. Tim Clark handles an American marten during his research in Wyoming.

This may be the only view forest visitors see of martens, which are secret and solitary hunters.

It's true—seeing a wild American marten is as much a prize today as a marten pelt was during the early fur trade. If you walk deep into an old evergreen forest, get off the roads, and keep very quiet, you just might see a flash of glossy fur as one chases a screeching red squirrel through the shadowy branches and disappears into a hole to eat it.

Although the marten has vanished from some of its former range, it is not a rare species. In fact, it is still an important commercial furbearer, especially in Canada. But its elusive habits are legendary, and it typically moves out of woodlands frequented by people. Naturalist Ernest Thompson Seton wrote in the early years of this century,

> Although I have spent, all told, many years in Marten country—in Ontario, Quebec, Manitoba, the Mackenzie, the Rockies, and the Sierra—I never but once saw a live free Marten. There can be little doubt that, during that time, a great many saw me, for the tracks were plentiful.

Let's see if we can keep the marten in sight long enough to discover the history and habits of this wilderness hunter.

1.

A Quizzical Face in a Gorgeous Fur Coat

Among the carnivores, meat-eating animals, is the large and fascinating family of mustelids, or weasel-like mammals. Mustelids are generally small to medium-sized animals with long, slender bodies, short legs, thick fur, and strong-smelling scent glands. They are curious, fast, and strong. Mustelids live on nearly every continent and have adapted to a wide range of habitats. Ground-dwelling ferrets and badgers are members of this tribe, along with their cousins, the skunks, the wolverines of the northern forests, and the fish-eating mink. Some otters, which live mostly in the water, are the largest mustelids. The least weasel, which prefers grassy areas, is the smallest. The American marten, an acrobat in the treetops, is one of the most beautiful.

The marten is a quick and agile hunter in the trees as well as on the ground.

This slender animal measures twenty-four to thirty inches long, one-third of which is its furry tail, important for balance and control in jumping. Martens usually weigh one to three pounds but may weigh as much as six. They are lean and muscular with very little body fat. The males are larger than the females, and martens in the north are generally larger than those in southern parts of their range.

Large rounded ears top their triangular faces. Vertical

The distinctive features of the marten are best seen up close.

"eyebrows" above the inner corners of their black eyes give them a quizzical look. Their powerful jaws and large canine teeth are adapted for eating meat, although they eat many other foods as well.

Compared to badgers or skunks, martens' short legs seem relatively long, and they bound in long strides. Their hind legs can be rotated 180 degrees, so they can grasp branches firmly and climb down trees headfirst. Specialized muscles and flexible spines make them amazingly agile and graceful. In fact, when they fall, they land on all fours like a cat. They walk on their toes, of which they have five on each foot with claws that partly retract like a cat's.

The martens' finest feature is their rich, lustrous brown fur, which is most beautiful in late fall. The deep, soft, woolly underfur is covered with stiff, glossy guard hairs. Their legs and tails are generally darker and their heads lighter. Individuals vary, however—some are all black, all white, or very dark brown. Completely yellow martens are called "canaries" in the fur trade. Contrasting

The American marten is a medium-sized mustelid.

The fisher, largest member of the genus Martes, *may weigh as much as twelve pounds. Like the marten, it has been reintroduced into parts of its former range.*

splotches of fur on their throats range from lemon-yellow to brilliant orange. In summer, their coats are dull and rough-looking; in winter, they do not turn white as weasels do.

The American marten, known to science as *Martes americana*, has seven close cousins—six other marten species and one fisher. All seven of these bushy-tailed species are similar to the American marten, although some are larger, some smaller. They are generally brown, sometimes black, with paler bibs of yellow, orange, or white. All live in forests, usually evergreen but also hardwood and tropical mountain forests. The sable, prized for its sumptuous fur, lives in northern Asia. The pine marten, whose name is sometimes used for the American marten, is found in northern Europe and western Asia. Southern Europe and central Asia are home to the stone marten. The yellow-throated marten lives in southeast Asia. Southern India is the native land of the Nilgiri marten, and the Japanese marten is found in Japan, of course, but also in Korea. The largest member of the family and the only other North American species, distinguished by its skill in eating porcupines, is the fisher.

2.

At Home in the Northern Forests

American martens live in the deep, evergreen forests all across northern North America. They range from the Atlantic Ocean to the Pacific, north to the tundra where there are no trees, and south to New England, the Great Lakes, the Rocky Mountains, and the Sierra Nevada Mountains in California.

Spruce, fir, hemlock, and pine trees make up the northern evergreen forests. Martens do best in *old* forests. There, towering trees and a thick canopy of branches keep the forest floor dark and damp—ideal for many small animals that martens eat. They also hide martens from their predators and keep the snow from piling up too deeply. Old forests have many layers and forms of life. They are full of leaning and fallen trees, stumps, logs

The old northern evergreen forest is a rich environment for many plants and animals.

rotting on the ground, and hollow dead trees—their insides killed by insects or fire. Mosses, lichens, and mushrooms flourish, and thickets of shrubs, ferns, and vines tangle around them. Seedlings sprout from the musty forest floor littered with dried grasses, needles, and leaf mold.

Although old evergreen forests are best, American martens can survive in other forest types, such as young evergreens, young or old hardwood forests, swamps, or mixed woods. They avoid open areas with no trees, especially in winter, but may use bogs and meadows if there are good places to get under the crusty snow. In summer, martens may hunt in rock slides and brushy fields if food and cover are available.

From this description of where martens live, we see an interesting fact: that *the structure of the environment* matters to martens. The numbers and kinds of trees and logs and

Dead trees are important resting and nesting places for martens.

shrubs and how they are arranged in the forest are just as important as how much food is there. An animal's habitat provides its "necessities of life." The marten's habitat includes, of course, food and water, but also certain kinds of places that fit its unique needs and abilities—hiding places, hunting sites, den sites, resting places.

Snow and cold are powerful forces in the north, where winter may last from October 1 to May 1. It is a critical season for all creatures, but northern animals—and even plants—have evolved many ways to cope with its forces. Martens are well adapted to staying active year-round. The soles of their feet are furry in winter, not only keeping them warmer but also acting as big, soft snowshoes. They are experts at taking advantage of natural snow formations—the hollows around stumps and leaning trees and under shrubs—to get to the mice under the snow. Since martens don't use the same den all the time, the cold forces them to keep warm in all sorts of little, insulated nooks. They may snooze in a cozy old squirrel nest, or wait out a blizzard in a hollow log or under a tree root. Snow is a good insulator, too, and curled up in natural snow caves, martens can stay toasty warm.

A furry American marten bounds easily through deep snow.

Here, a marten leaves one of the natural openings to the hunting grounds under the snow. Mice move about freely in an icy, open lattice - work that forms in the snow just above ground level.

With so little fat, martens can't "hole up" for long periods—they must hunt and eat often. They tunnel through snow, bound along trails made by other animals, and use fallen logs as runways. They need networks of logs and brush piles to hunt in, leaning trees to climb and watch from, a canopy of treetops to chase squirrels in, and thick bushes of juicy berries to eat.

A fallen log acts as a micro-environment. The rotting wood feeds insects, the roots and insect holes harbor small animals, and the log becomes a runway and lookout point for hunting martens.

When the old forests are destroyed, marten habitat is also ruined for many years. Fires may kill the big trees and burn up the old, decayed logs as well as the greenery. A few deer mice and chipmunks can live on the dry forest floor after a fire, but they are not the best foods for martens. People also destroy forests. In the centuries since North America was first settled, vast forests have been cut down—at first to clear away the "dark and dangerous" features of a new and unknown continent, and later to

A fire can burn thousands of acres of forest habitat—home to many animals.

provide lumber for building, to clear land for farming, and to build roads. Martens can tolerate some minor disturbances to their environment. They may even live near people's houses if the forest still surrounds them and if enough food is still available.

Although it is a demanding environment, many other forest dwellers call these northern regions home. Tree squirrels chatter in the highest branches and shred thousands of spruce cones to nibble the seeds. At night, flying squirrels glide noiselessly from tree to tree, and great gray owls swoop down. Millions of mice and voles

Here, the heartwood of a large tree was excavated and the hole used as a den by a marten.

and chipmunks live on or under the ground or in the trees. Moose wade in the shallow ponds dammed up by industrious beavers. Woodland caribou, elk, and deer are alerted by the squawking of jays. Ruffed grouse, red squirrels, and wood ducks are among the many species that, like martens, need old evergreen forests. Martens are part of this complex community of hundreds of living plants and animals. It is a community with subtle and intricate bonds, and every species has its own role in it.

Some other predators compete with martens for food: lynx, fishers and wolverines, wolves and foxes and coyotes, bears, hawks and eagles and owls, weasels and mink. But each species seems to have a special advantage in certain times and places so that the competition doesn't get too direct or too intense. Martens have several advantages.

The great horned owl is one of the many predators that compete with martens for small prey.

Although still in the nest, this young hawk will become one of the many competitors for small mammals.

They can hunt in either day or night, and they can hunt high in the evergreens, on the ground, or under the snow. As medium-sized hunters, they can take prey which is too large for some predators and too small for others. Some of the larger carnivores may try to catch martens for food, but the fast and agile martens are seldom taken.

3.

The Ways of a Hunter

What moss is to the Reindeer, what grass is to the Buffalo, the Mouse millions of the North are to all the Northern carnivores from Bear to Blarina.... We shall for each of these flesh-eaters write, "It sometimes eats this and sometimes eats that, but by far the greatest bulk of its food is Mice."

This is eminently true of the Marten. Its diet comprises partridge, Rabbits, Squirrels, Chipmunks, Shrews, and Mice; birds, birds' eggs, fledglings, frogs, toads, fish, insects, and Mice; but it also adds reptiles, nuts, berries, honey, carrion— and Mice.

ERNEST THOMPSON SETON

Across their entire North American range, martens eat small mammals more than any other food. One staple is the red-backed vole, which requires the fallen trees and damp conditions of uncut, unburned evergreen forests. All varieties of squirrels may be eaten. Chipmunks, field mice, jumping mice, pocket gophers, lemmings, and muskrats are additional rodent foods. Martens need about three mice per day, or the equivalent. The Cree Indian name for martens is "wabachis," meaning "rabbit chaser," which tells us that martens also hunt the snowshoe hares common in northern regions.

Martens are adaptable, unspecialized feeders. Their diets vary because some individuals seem to prefer some foods to others, and because different foods are available in different regions in different seasons. In the spring, martens add eggs and young, nesting birds to their diets. In summer, insects, earthworms, toads, frogs, lizards, and fish are available along with huckleberries, blueberries, cranberries, and strawberries. Nuts and seeds and wild rose hips are eaten in the fall. In winter, martens may eat carrion (animals which have died from disease, predators, or other causes). How much food is available determines how often they must forage. There is a critical balance between the energy martens receive from their food and

The chickaree, a common winter prey of martens along the West Coast, stores piles of cones and nuts, which may be raided by martens for food.

The flying squirrel is another marten prey that requires evergreen forests.

the energy they must spend in hunting for it. Rarely is there any excess energy to be stored as fat.

"Greased lightning aloft" is how one writer described martens. Their tree-climbing agility is second to none, but martens do most of their hunting on the ground. They can

Martens can bound quickly through branches and brush.

Walking is not a common gait for martens—bounding, leaping, scrambling, and climbing are more likely means to a meal.

cover long distances in a day. They explore in a zigzag pattern, investigating every crevice and hole, every brush pile or branch for hidden prey. They dive into dense, tangled clumps and emerge suddenly to bound quickly to the next likely hunting site.

Their hunting tactics are many. Sometimes martens slowly follow the tracks of their prey, sniffing and looking. Sometimes they stalk unsuspecting animals, lie flat behind a ledge or log to wait, and finally lunge and chase them. If a leaping rush at a brush pile doesn't scare out any mice, they may proceed to probe every crack and hollow. They may stand on their hind legs or climb three feet up a tree to scan below for signs of small animals,

Here, a marten peeks out from under a log where it has been hunting. The tiny eartags identify it as one of the martens from Tim Clark's study area.

pounce on them, then perch and pounce again. They may bite and claw at holes in the dirt or in trees to reach hidden prey. Sometimes they stay at the sites of kills for a few days, and sometimes they carry food back to their dens or resting sites, peering out alertly many times while they eat. They can swim, if necessary.

4.

The Social Life
of a Lone Predator

Martens first mate when they are one or two years old. Mating is a tense time for these otherwise solitary carnivores. When individuals meet in the wild during most of the year, they growl and back away. But during the mating season, they change their behavior and come together without attacking one another. Ritualized playing, mutual grooming, and living and sleeping together for a couple of weeks help males and females to overcome their unsocial tendencies. After mating in July or August, they resume their solitary lives.

After the long, severe winter, the mother gives birth in April. A litter usually has three babies, but may range from one to six. The one-ounce newborns are blind, deaf,

The large dark clump near the top of the photo is dwarf mistletoe, also called a witch's broom. This is a good nest site for a marten family in a dense forest.

and helpless. Thin yellow fuzz covers their tiny bodies. The mother keeps them safe from predators in a den high in a hollow tree, with the nest lined with grass, leaves, or moss to keep them warm. Their ears open when they are 3½ weeks old, and their eyes finally open to their treetop world when they are 5½ weeks old.

Their youth is a time of learning how to survive, for, although martens may live to be fifteen, nearly all their lives will be spent alone with no one to help or to teach them. What kind of survival training prepares these youngsters? Play! Few of us realize that play is important work, but it is, and martens are very playful. From their first days in the nest, they smell and pat and shake everything around them. As they grow, they begin tumbling, scratching, and biting. They communicate through growls, huffs, pants, chuckles, and *eeps*. By 6½ weeks, they are very active. The mother then moves them one-by-one to a new den at ground level. Then, when they start chasing and jumping and exploring, they won't fall out of the tree. Through play, young martens become physically fit and learn to control their legs and tails and paws. They are born with powerful instincts to catch and kill prey, and play provides a harmless outlet for these developing skills. Play also helps them learn about each other and keeps them occupied together while their mother hunts.

A marten mother has important responsibilities toward her kits: to feed and care for them, protect them, and teach them to survive in the wild. At first, she feeds her young only milk from her body. After a few weeks, she brings prey back to the den for them. She weans them when they are six weeks old, but they still depend on her to bring them food. Eventually, she carries live prey to the nest and waits for them to kill and eat it themselves. She doesn't actually "teach" them, but provides situations in which they can practice and perfect their instincts. Later, when they can leave the den, they travel with her while she hunts and, by doing what she does, they learn to stalk and pounce and catch animals.

By late summer, they are practiced hunters. Their bodies are as long as an adult's and their teeth are fully developed, but they will continue to put on weight for several more months. They are ready to survive on their own and gradually leave their mother and littermates to

A young marten explores the edge of a stream...

. . . and then dries itself in the sun.

Young martens are at home in the treetops.

live alone. At this time, their mother is ready to mate again and prepare for her next family.

The marten community is always changing. Some "residents" will live in the same area for many years. Others stay only a short time. Each marten tries to establish its own territory—an area of land and trees to provide all its needs. They mark the boundaries with a musky fluid from glands on their bellies to warn other martens of the same sex to stay out. They defend their territories by growling and baring their teeth, chasing, biting, and wrestling. Males defend large territories of two to six square miles against other males. Females use smaller areas overlapping the males' territories, and defend them from other females. Adults tolerate young martens that are leaving their mothers' territories and traveling far to find unclaimed areas to establish their own territories.

Because people are sociable creatures, it is hard for us to understand the solitary life of martens. But this kind of life has a great advantage for them. The biggest danger to martens is not predators or disease. It is the unpredictable amount of food and the great difficulties of hunting in this harsh land. Thus, staying strictly separated gives each marten its own special hunting place. If the habitat has lots of food and hunting places and if there are not too many other martens to compete with, then each marten will do well on a small territory. But in poor habitat, martens may need very large territories in order to get enough food, and fewer martens can live in the area. Females suffer most in poor habitats because they are smaller and also bear and raise the young.

This old male will defend his territory against other male martens.

5.

"Fine Furres & Precious Skinnes"

Furs were the first clothes of prehistoric people. Even after the development of weaving, fine fabrics were trimmed with fur to add warmth and beauty. Martens have always been among the most valuable furs, reserved for kings and noblemen and churchmen. In the eleventh century, a geographer described the Prussians as "setting little value on gold and silver, but much more on their store of furs, and especially on their marten skins."

Furs were so highly prized that the desire for them greatly affected the history of the world. By the time of the Middle Ages, people had been hunting animals in Europe for furs, leather, and food for centuries, and the numbers of wild animals had dwindled. By the 1300s, the only remaining deer were in royal preserves and could not be

47

The luxurious fur of the American marten gleams in the sunlight.

hunted by common people. Within a hundred years, there were not enough native furbearing animals to meet the needs of western Europe. By the time of the Renaissance, the demand for furs was enormous!

Trade for furs began, first in Scandinavia, eastern Europe, and Russia. But even the Russian supply of furbearers was exhausted by the end of the 1500s, and the czar commissioned the cossacks from the Black Sea to trap furbearers east to the Pacific Ocean. By the 1700s, the Russians were trapping in Alaska. The discovery of the New World led trappers west across the Atlantic Ocean, too. They came with the explorers and fishermen and missionaries and those seeking gold and riches and a short route to the Far East. The New World fur trade helped to supply Europe's needs. It yielded great riches to the businessmen who set up trading companies which bought furs from trappers and Indians and sold them in Europe. Eventually, the fur trade spanned the continent, and business continued to grow throughout the eighteenth and nineteenth centuries.

Early trappers met many groups of North American Indians and learned that furs were equally precious to these people. The Indians used native furs for clothing and equipment. They built homes with skins and furnished them with furs. Furs were used as money to trade for other goods, and tribes sometimes even fought over hunting

This 1612 map by explorer Samuel de Champlain shows a section of the eastern Great Lakes where the fur trade was an important reason for exploration. The marten, labeled martre, *appears in the center at the bottom. (From The Works of Samuel de Champlain, Plate LXXXI, The Champlain Society.)*

grounds. Furbearing animals populated Indian myths about spiritual and worldly matters.

The fur trade was a colorful period in North America's history. Hardy, adventuresome men explored and lived off the land. In the East, French-Canadian boatmen paddled birchbark canoes into remote regions and returned to the trading posts heavily loaded with bales of furs. In the West, mountain men trapped alone all year through the Rockies and gathered in the spring for boisterous meetings. The Hudson's Bay Company, started in 1670, had trading posts over most of what is now Canada. Other big fur companies also conducted business in the "peltry," or furs, of North America.

The American marten was a very valuable furbearer, second only to beavers in the amount of money it provided to the traders.

The vast North American fur trade had consequences beyond the boundaries of Canada and the United States. Nearly all of Europe and Asia, and even faraway China, were connected in the complex web of trading deals based on furs. The fur trade influenced government policies on commerce and land and dealings with the Indians. It produced diplomatic crises and wars for control of trapping grounds. It created fortunes for a lucky few and a new level of commerce throughout the world. It changed the wilderness through exploration and colonization, and it was a major cause of the tragic destruction of Indian peoples and their cultures.

The fur trade slowed in the mid-nineteenth century. The animals on which the trade depended were depleted. Settlements were creeping west. And at last, as clothing fashions changed and good, cheap cloth became more widely available, the demand for furs decreased.

6.

Conservation and Management

In the last 150 years, concern for the conservation of wild animals has grown. People generally agree now that the goal of conservation is "wise use" of animals and their habitats, but there is an ongoing debate on how exactly to define and achieve "wise use." Many groups of people are involved in the debate. Lawmakers decide on policies and assign money to conservation programs, while administrators direct the programs and wardens enforce the laws. Scientists conduct research to discover biological facts. Managers manipulate animal populations and their habitats based on these facts and on the goals set by society. Educators inform the public. The last but biggest group is the many thousands of people who enjoy and use and care about wildlife—bird watchers, photographers,

53

Martens have benefitted from much research attention in the past few decades.

hunters, tourists, outfitters, landowners, hikers, fisher-men, nature lovers, and artists. All these people, in turn, influence the conservation process by giving their ideas and opinions to the lawmakers and planners.

Naturalist Aldo Leopold defined conservation as "man living in harmony with the land." Many other human uses of the land compete with wildlife, but most activities can continue while animals and habitat are protected at the same time. Ninety-nine percent of the earth's land does not have complete protection for native animals and plants, and it will take imagination and long-term planning to conserve species and achieve harmony.

Conservation and management of furbearing animals, including martens, is an especially stubborn challenge for two reasons. First, too many martens are trapped when the price of the fur is high, while few are trapped when the price is low. This leads to greater population swings than is healthy for the marten populations. Second, trapping is a controversial issue. The steel leg-hold traps cause cruel, painful deaths of the martens, and thus many people protest against the use of fur products.

With regard to martens, conservation and management

Live trapping does not harm the animals, and it provides important information to biologists about the health of the animals, the size of their territories, and how long they live in an area.

have two goals. The first is to safeguard marten populations. One way to do this is to maintain refuges where no martens are trapped; dispersing martens from the refuges can repopulate nearby areas. Also, martens can be transplanted from healthy populations to areas where they no longer live, but where there is suitable habitat. But the best way to manage marten populations is to manage the people who trap them. Managers may limit trapping to certain seasons, or to certain numbers, ages, or sexes of martens. They may limit how close traps can be placed to each other. In some states or provinces, trappers must take a class to learn about martens and how to trap them most humanely. Sometimes, when a marten population is in danger, managers cancel trapping altogether.

Protecting marten habitat is the second, equally important goal of conservation and management. It may take a hundred to two hundred years to regrow a forest where martens can thrive, and so, in our many activities in the forests, we must consider martens' special habitat needs. Foresters can limit or avoid "clear cuts," a logging practice which cuts down *all* the trees in an area. They can cut some of the trees, but leave the biggest ones with holes and thick branches for martens and other animals. They can also leave all the dead, leaning, and fallen trees and piles of broken branches. An excellent method is to leave some parts of the old evergreen forests intact and not to permit any logging at all. Foresters can even manage forest fires to favor marten habitat: burning small areas on purpose opens up space on the ground for shrubs and helps prevent

Chain saws are one of the many machines people use in logging. After the trees are cut, heavy equipment—skidders, bulldozers, and trucks—are brought in to drag the trees to a loading area, hoist them onto trucks, and build roads to haul them out.

One result of limited logging which can benefit many forest species is "slash piles" of all the branches and litter. In early days, the piles were burned, but now they are left as habitat for many small mammals and their predators.

big fires which would kill everything. Foresters can also limit road building and land clearing, prevent people from visiting some forests, and allow insects to kill some trees to create new holes and food for martens.

Recently, in some forests, managers are viewing martens as an "indicator species," that is, as a barometer or index of the overall health of the whole community. Martens may be a good indicator species for the old northern evergreen forest because they are so sensitive to disturbances in the forest community. Changes in marten populations may reveal the effects of management actions on many additional species—other predators, many prey species, and the plants themselves.

This idea reflects a growing trend toward conserving whole, natural communities. People are letting go of old ideas of manipulating wildlife to serve their desires. The American marten will benefit from this more comprehensive approach to nature. We will see the martens' many other values, besides as a commercial furbearer. Martens

Martens are a symbol of our wildlife heritage and a sign of our stewardship of the forests.

have a biological value in their role in evergreen forest ecology, consuming rodents and carrion. They have a scientific value as researchers discover the processes that regulate their populations and their sensitive responses to the health of the forests. But for most of us, they will just mean lots of fun hiking with binoculars, cameras, and sketchbooks, trying to catch a glimpse of one of the loveliest sights in the forest—the American marten.

Index

Page numbers in *italic* indicate photographs